EDGE
BOOKS™

ALL
ABOUT
DOGS

BEAGLES

by Tammy Gagne

Consultant: Dr. Emily W. B. Southgate
Certified Senior Ecologist and Life-long Beagler
National Beagle Club of America

Capstone

Mankato, Minnesota

Edge Books are published by Capstone Press,
151 Good Counsel Drive, P.O. Box 669, Mankato, Minnesota 56002.
www.capstonepress.com

Books published by Capstone Press are manufactured with paper
containing at least 10 percent post-consumer waste.

Library of Congress Cataloging-in-Publication Data
Gagne, Tammy.
    Beagles / by Tammy Gagne.
    p. cm. — (Edge books. All about dogs)
    Includes bibliographical references and index.
    Summary: "Describes the history, physical features, temperament, and care
of the beagle breed" — Provided by publisher.
    ISBN 978-1-4296-3366-6 (library binding)
    1. Beagle (Dog breed) — Juvenile literature. I. Title.
SF429.B3G34 2010
636.753'7 — dc22   2008055921

Editorial Credits
Jennifer Besel and Molly Kolpin, editors; Veronica Bianchini, designer;
    Marcie Spence, media researcher

Photo Credits
Alamy/Brian Elliott, 17
Capstone Press/Karon Dubke, cover, 1, 19, 20–21, 22, 24, 27
Dreamstime/Percho, 16
Getty Images Inc./Christopher Furlong, 10–11
iStockphoto/princessdlaf, 29
Mary Evans Picture Library, 9
Ron Kimball Stock/Ron Kimball, 6
Shutterstock/Charlene Bayerle, 23; Connie Wade, 14; Michal Napartowicz, 13;
    TheSupe87, 25; verityjohnson, 5, 7

Table of Contents

CHAPTER 1

A FUN FRIEND

Beagles and children go together like peanut butter and jelly. You have probably seen beagles in movies, cartoons, or comic strips. Almost always, the beagles are running alongside boys and girls. When these dogs aren't playing, they are hunting. They sniff out animal tracks with their amazing sense of smell.

Beagles are energetic dogs. This trait makes the **breed** a great pet for active people. To work off all that energy, beagles need plenty of space to run and play.

Because beagles love kids, they make excellent family pets. Beagles are tough enough to handle some rough play, but kids should always treat dogs with respect.

breed — a certain kind of animal within an animal group

Beagles are playful, fun-loving dogs.

Breeders can help match you with a puppy that fits your personality.

EDGE FACT

One of the most famous beagles of all time is Snoopy, from the *Peanuts* comic strip drawn by Charles Schulz.

Finding a Beagle

The best place to buy a beagle puppy is from a breeder. Good breeders raise healthy and friendly puppies.

You can find adult beagles through your local animal shelter or rescue group. Be just as picky when adopting an adult beagle as you would be when buying a puppy. Most beagles have friendly personalities, but every dog is a little different. If you take your time, you will find the perfect dog for you.

CHAPTER 2

BEAGLE HISTORY

The exact beginnings of the beagle aren't known for sure. Hounds that hunt in packs have existed in England for more than 2,000 years. These ancient hounds are thought to be the ancestors of today's beagles. By the 1300s, King Edward III of England was using small hunting dogs that looked similar to the beagles we know today.

Early beagles were used to hunt **hares**. The beagle's small size, endless energy, and sensitive nose all made it perfect for this job. Although most hunting was done on horseback, hunters worked with beagles on foot. Hunting with beagles is called beagling.

By the 1700s, fox hunting was popular in England. Owners bred large buck hounds with early beagles to produce foxhounds. Today's beagles look a lot like foxhounds, only smaller.

hare — an animal that looks like a large rabbit with long, strong back legs

Because of their good sense of smell and small size, early beagles were perfect for hunting hares.

In the United States

In the 1800s, small hunting dogs called beagles also lived in the United States. But these dogs looked more like basset hounds and dachshunds, with longer bodies and shorter legs than the beagle we know today. But the 1860s brought a big change. English beagles were bred with U.S. beagles to create a true breed type. This breeding created the beagle we now know and love.

Beagles are still used for hunting in both the United States and England. They are often champions in field trials. In these events, dogs are awarded points for hunting ability.

EDGE FACT

Former U.S. President Lyndon Baines Johnson owned three beagles. Their names were Him, Her, and Edgar.

Dogs that closely match the breed standard compete in dog shows.

CHAPTER 3

FRiENDLY AND SMART

The beagle has been among the most popular dogs in the United States for nearly a century. It is easy to understand why. The beagle is good-looking, friendly, and smart.

Physical Features

Beagles can be many colors. Most beagles are tricolored dogs. These beagles are black, tan, and white. Their **saddles** are black. They have white legs and stomachs and tan heads. They also have tan at the edge of their saddles and white on their muzzles.

Lemon and white beagles and red and white beagles are also common in the breed. The colors vary, but generally lemon and white dogs are white with light tan. Red and white dogs have a red-brown saddle on a white body.

saddle — a colored marking on the back of a dog

Some beagles are called tricolored because their coats have three colors.

EDGE FACT

Tricolored beagles are born black and white. The tan color develops slowly as the puppies get older.

Most people can tell a beagle from other breeds when they see its floppy ears. A beagle's long ears should lie close to its head.

Beagles' eyes are brown or a golden-brown color called hazel. They are large and set far apart on the dog's head.

Beagles are divided into two types for dog shows. One type includes dogs measuring 13 inches (33 centimeters) or less at the top of their shoulders. Beagles taller than 13 inches (33 centimeters) but no more than 15 inches (38 centimeters) make up the second variety. Beagles standing taller than 15 inches (38 centimeters) cannot compete in American Kennel Club (AKC) dog shows. Dogs of all sizes are born in the same litters.

Big eyes and long ears give the beagle a kind expression.

Temperament

Beagles are social animals. They do best in households with other dogs. Two beagles will keep each other company when family members aren't home. Many beagles also live peacefully with cats, but others chase them. To some beagles, a cat is just as much fun to chase as a rabbit.

This breed adores people. Your beagle will always be the first to welcome visitors through the door. Just be sure everyone who enters the door closes it behind them. Even a well-trained beagle will follow its hunting **instinct** and run outside if a squirrel catches its eye.

Although some people keep beagles as outdoor pets, a beagle should live inside whenever possible. If left outside alone, this breed will follow any scent that attracts its powerful nose. And don't expect a fence to keep your beagle where it belongs. A beagle that is eager to follow a trail may dig to the point of escape.

Beagles love to follow scents, even if they have to dig to find the source.

instinct — behavior that is natural rather than learned

Beagles get along with other dogs very well.

Beagles don't drool or have a doggy odor. But they will smell bad if they roll in something stinky.

CHAPTER 4

CARING FOR A BEAGLE

Beagles can make excellent pets. They enjoy being with their owners, but they don't require loads of care like many other breeds. Still, owning any dog is a big responsibility.

Training

Beagles need basic **obedience** training. Start by teaching your dog to sit and stay on command. Obedience classes can help you train your dog. These classes can be fun for both you and your dog. When training is fun, dogs learn more quickly.

Schedule several short training sessions each day. Sessions should last no longer than five or 10 minutes. If the session is too long, your beagle will get bored. If you wait too long between sessions, your dog may forget what it has already learned. The key to successful training is holding your dog's attention. Giving your beagle treats as rewards usually helps.

obedience — following rules and commands

For a well-behaved dog, work on training every day.

Before bringing your beagle home, find out what type of food the dog has been eating. Continue feeding your beagle the same food until your pet settles into its new home. After a few weeks, you can start switching your dog to a different type of food if you need to. It is best to make diet changes slowly. Sudden changes can upset dogs' stomachs.

Beagle puppies should eat puppy food until they are about six months old. Pet supply stores have many types of puppy and adult dog food. You can even buy special food for active dogs or overweight pets.

Most beagles only need two meals each day. Dogs that are overfed can become overweight. Beagles are active, but they can still become overweight. Overweight dogs are much more likely to get sick than trim dogs.

High-quality dog food will help keep your beagle healthy.

Exercise

Beagles need regular exercise to stay healthy and happy. Remember, these dogs were bred to hunt. Take your dog on a brisk walk at least once each day. If you jog, you can take your adult beagle with you. Start by running with your dog for short distances. Then work up to running more often and for longer time periods.

Beagles enjoy walks with their owners.

Chasing a ball is a great way for your dog to work off some energy.

Younger dogs need regular but less demanding exercise. A young beagle's growing bones are more easily injured than an adult's. Wait until your dog is at least one year old before jogging with it.

Exercise time can also be playtime. Toys like balls and flying discs make exercise fun. Play with your beagle in your own backyard or at a local dog park.

Grooming

Beagles' short fur doesn't become tangled. Beagles do need to be brushed about once a week, though. Brushing removes dirt and dead hair from your dog's coat.

If you brush your dog regularly, it won't need a bath more than once every month or two. But remember that many beagles like to dig in the dirt outside. If your dog does this, start running the bath water and reach for the dog shampoo.

Beagles have longer eyelashes than many other dog breeds. Check your dog's lashes regularly, and trim them if necessary. If left too long, eyelashes can interfere with your dog's vision or even injure its eyes.

Nail and dental care is also important for your dog. Trim your beagle's toenails every few weeks. Brush your dog's teeth as often as possible. Daily brushing is best, but even once a week will help prevent plaque and tartar from forming.

Bathing and brushing help keep your dog's coat clean and shiny.

Veterinary Care

Take your beagle to its veterinarian for a checkup at least once a year. The vet will check your dog's weight, take its temperature, and give it any necessary **vaccinations**.

Like all breeds, beagles are more likely to have certain health problems. The eyes and back are often what cause beagles the most trouble.

Older beagles may suffer from **cataracts**, which make it difficult for the dog to see clearly. A vet can perform surgery to remove cataracts. During this operation, the vet replaces the dog's natural eye lens with a manufactured lens.

Many beagles also suffer from disk problems in their backs. Like humans, a dog's spine has many flat pieces called disks. When a disk slips out of place, it can be very painful. Dogs often need surgery to correct this problem.

EDGE FACT

Healthy beagles can live up to 15 years.

vaccination — a shot of medicine that protects animals from a disease

cataract — a cloudy spot that can form on the lens of a beagle's eye

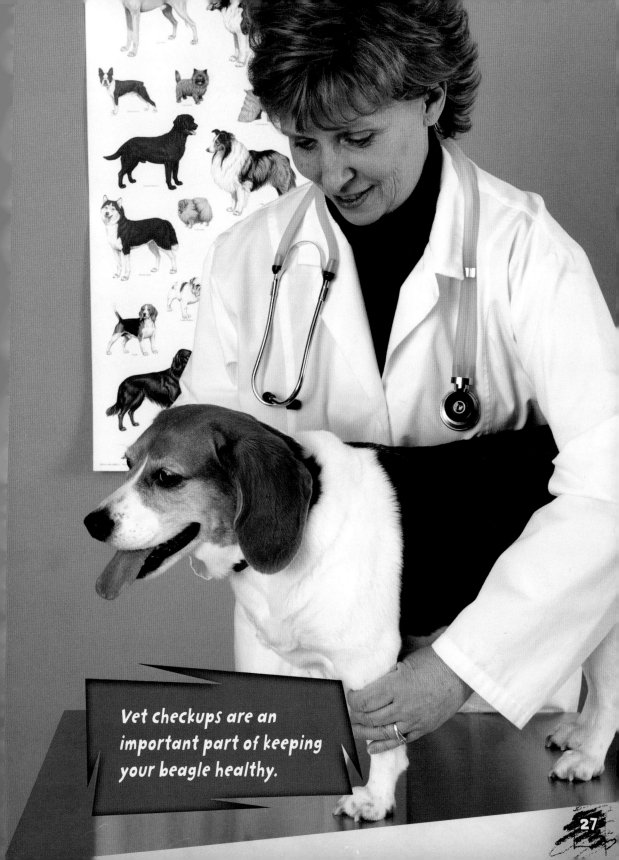

Vet checkups are an important part of keeping your beagle healthy.

Not all health problems can be prevented, but most can be treated. The key is catching a problem early. If your beagle has cloudy eyes or seems to be in pain, bring it to the vet as soon as possible. Vets may also be able to detect illnesses in their early stages during routine checkups.

At your dog's first checkup, talk to your vet about **spaying** or **neutering** your dog. These simple operations help control the pet population. These operations can also reduce a dog's risk for some types of cancer.

A Floppy-Eared Friend

Caring for a beagle isn't difficult, and it comes with many rewards. Good care will help your dog live a long, healthy life. In return, your beagle will provide you with many years of love, loyalty, and laughs.

spay — an operation that prevents a female dog from producing offspring

neuter — an operation that prevents a male dog from producing offspring

A healthy beagle can be part of your life for many years.

Glossary

breed (BREED) — a certain kind of animal within an animal group; breed also means to mate and raise a certain kind of animal

cataract (KA-tuh-rakt) — a cloudy spot that can form on the lens of a beagle's eye

hare (HAIR) — an animal that looks like a large rabbit with long, strong back legs

instinct (IN-stingkt) — behavior that is natural rather than learned

neuter (NOO-tur) — a veterinary operation that prevents a male dog from producing offspring

obedience (oh-BEE-dee-uhnss) — obeying rules and commands

saddle (SAD-uhl) — a colored marking on the back of a dog

spay (SPEY) — a veterinary operation that prevents a female dog from producing offspring

vaccination (vak-suh-NAY-shun) — a shot of medicine that protects animals from a disease

Read More

Gray, Susan H. *Beagles*. Domestic Dogs. Mankato, Minn.: Child's World, 2008.

Landau, Elaine. *Beagles are the Best!* The Best Dogs Ever. Minneapolis: Lerner, 2010.

Palika, Liz, and Katherine A. Miller. *Animals at Work*. ASPCA Kids. Hoboken, N.J.: Wiley, 2009.

Internet Sites

FactHound offers a safe, fun way to find Internet sites related to this book. All of the sites on FactHound have been researched by our staff.

Here's all you do:

Visit *www.facthound.com*

FactHound will fetch the best sites for you!

Index